Art Director   Charles Matheson
Art Editor   Ben White
Designer   Malcolm Smythe
Editor   Jill Hughes
Researcher   Dee Robinson
Consultant   W P Escreet
     (Lecturer in Aerodynamics,
     City University, London)

Illustrators   Denis Bishop
        Peter Holt
        Industrial Art Studios

First published 1982 by
William Collins Sons & Co Ltd

Copyright © Aladdin Books Ltd 1982

Printed in Belgium

ISBN 0 00 195374 5

Contents

The Inside Story

JETLINER

FROM TAKEOFF TO TOUCHDOWN

Chris Chant

COLLINS

The Airport

Flight 010 is a ten-hour transatlantic journey from Miami to Frankfurt and is typical of many such long distance flights that are made daily all over the world. At the airline terminal passengers are arriving for their flights. Normal check-in time is at least one hour before departure and at the airline counter staff check the tickets, weigh the luggage and issue each passenger with a boarding card showing the seat number and departure gate. Each item of luggage is individually labelled by the staff and put on to moving escalators which take it to a central handling area. Here the luggage is sorted according to the flight number and loaded into containers.

When the flight is called, passengers proceed from the central lounge across to the individual departure gate. Although in this case there is no passport control when leaving the USA, in most other countries it is a standard procedure. Before entering the departure lounge all passengers and their hand baggage are thoroughly searched for hidden weapons.

In the foreground being prepared for the flight is a giant Boeing 747 or Jumbo – the largest of the wide bodied aircraft. Containers with the luggage and additional freight are lifted into the holds, and the ground crew make last minute checks to the tyres and engines. In the cockpit the flight crew are starting their preflight checks.

The flight is ready for boarding. Passengers with seat numbers at the rear of the aircraft proceed first and passing through the walkway are greeted by the cabin crew and shown to their seats.

Attached to the departure lounge is a mobile walkway which extends up against the main jetliner door. The terminal itself consists of many such lounges and gates, and is situated near the centre of the runway complex. It is surrounded by airport offices, hangars, a freight centre, control tower, flight operations building, emergency services and a weather office.

The anatomy of an airport:
1 Car parks; 2 Airline courtesy bus;
3 Airport and flight information desks;
4 Ticket sales; 5 Car and hotel reservations; 6 Flight observation lounge; 7 Baggage weigh-in;
8 Passenger and ticket check-in; 9 Passport control; 10 Security officials;
11 Duty-free shopping centre;
12 Transit lounges; 13 Boarding gates;
14 Mobile walkways; 15 Baggage handling; 16 Airport service vehicles;
17 Commissary truck (aircraft cleaning and catering); 18 Airport freight vehicles; 19 Freight security checks; 20 Control Tower; 21 Airport offices; 22 Airport emergency service vehicles; 23 Aircraft park and servicing areas; 24 Runway;
25 Aircraft taxiways.

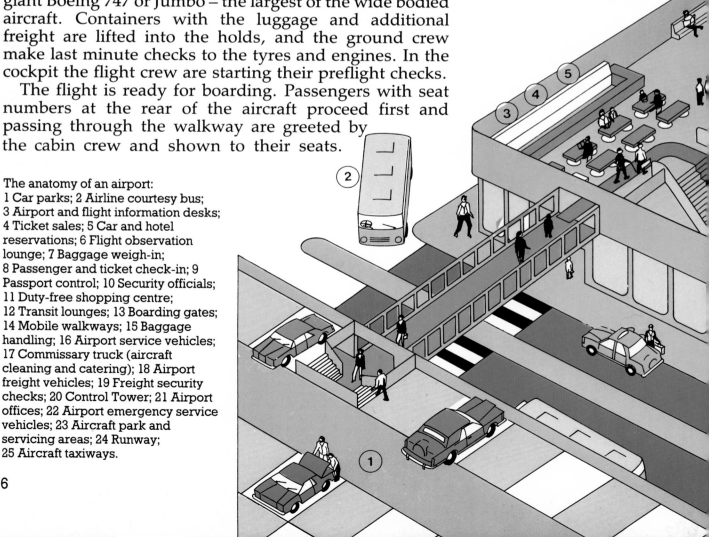

Taking Off

The cabin crew check that all the passengers are on board, and the doors are closed and locked. Gently the walkway swings back from the fuselage – the body of the jetliner – and a specially designed tractor pushes the giant 747 away from the loading bay. Meanwhile, the Airport Traffic Control has given clearance to start the engines and the flight crew carry out all the last minute checks. All the systems are in full working order, and the wing flaps and flying controls are tested.

At the same time the cabin crew check that all the passengers are wearing their seat belts properly and then demonstrate the emergency procedures. They point out the exits on the jetliner, and demonstrate how to wear and inflate the lifejackets under each seat. Lastly they show how to use the oxygen masks which automatically fall from the ceiling should it become difficult for the passengers to breathe.

The aircraft shown in this picture is a Boeing 747-200B, the standard passenger version of the original Jumbo. It was the first, and still is, the largest of today's generation of widebodied jetliners that now include the DC10, TriStar and Airbus. Different versions of these aircraft are produced for short-haul, long-haul, freight, and a mixture of passenger and freight.

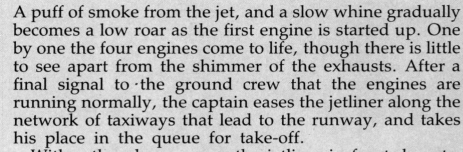

A puff of smoke from the jet, and a slow whine gradually becomes a low roar as the first engine is started up. One by one the four engines come to life, though there is little to see apart from the shimmer of the exhausts. After a final signal to ·the ground crew that the engines are running normally, the captain eases the jetliner along the network of taxiways that lead to the runway, and takes his place in the queue for take-off.

With a thunderous roar, the jetliner in front departs. With flaps fully extended for take-off the 747 turns onto the main runway. The pilot and co-pilot each place a hand firmly on the throttle levers, and push them steadily forward. The vibration and noise swells as the engines are brought up to full power. Suddenly the brakes are released, and the passengers are pressed back into their seats as all 313 tonnes of the Boeing 747 accelerate up the runway.

Regardless of fuel consumption and noise, the engines are operated at full power on take-off. The wing flaps are fully extended to 'increase' the size of the wing. This gives the maximum possible lift at a time when the aircraft is at its heaviest with a full load of 100 tonnes of fuel. Once the airliner is off the ground and has attained enough speed the flaps are drawn back into the wing.

The wing's special curved shape causes the air to flow faster over the upper surface than the lower surface. This reduces the pressure of the airflow over the upper surface, and lift is produced as the higher-pressure air under the wing attempts to equalize the pressures above.

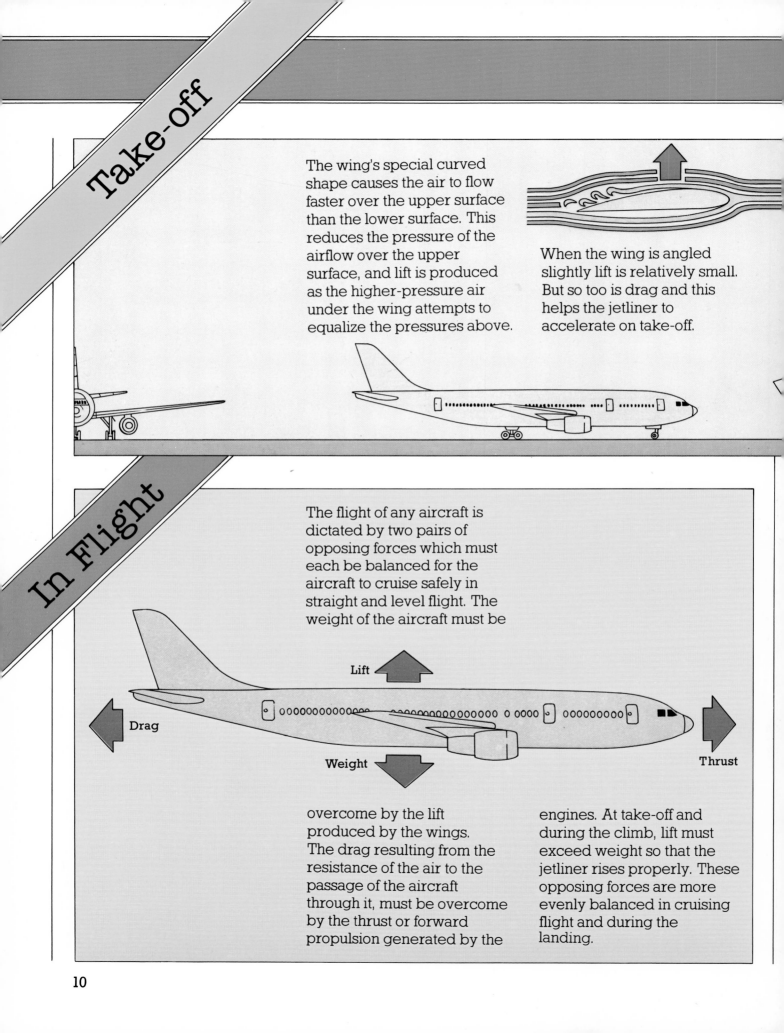

When the wing is angled slightly lift is relatively small. But so too is drag and this helps the jetliner to accelerate on take-off.

The flight of any aircraft is dictated by two pairs of opposing forces which must each be balanced for the aircraft to cruise safely in straight and level flight. The weight of the aircraft must be

Lift

Drag

Weight

Thrust

overcome by the lift produced by the wings. The drag resulting from the resistance of the air to the passage of the aircraft through it, must be overcome by the thrust or forward propulsion generated by the engines. At take-off and during the climb, lift must exceed weight so that the jetliner rises properly. These opposing forces are more evenly balanced in cruising flight and during the landing.

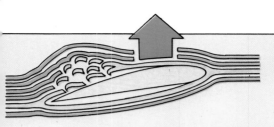

At take-off speed, the nose of the aircraft is pulled up and the sudden change in the wings' angle increases lift dramatically.

If the angle of the nose becomes too great a 'stall' can occur.

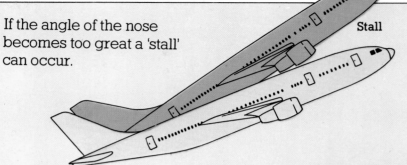

Stall

The upper surface airflow breaks away and lift is greatly reduced. This can cause the aircraft to stop flying if its airspeed is too low.

Controls

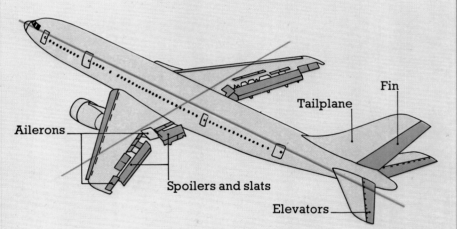

Ailerons

Spoilers and slats

Fin

Tailplane

Elevators

In flight an aircraft is controlled by the pilot in three ways. The elevators on the tailplane pitch the aircraft up or down and the rudder on the fin of the tailplane moves or 'yaws' the aircraft to the left or right. The ailerons – small flaps – on the wing control the 'roll'. Also located on the wing are a number of devices to improve (slats or flaps) or reduce (spoilers) the wing's lift.

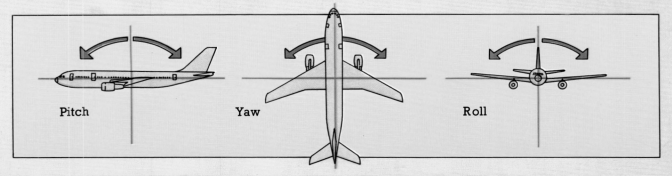

Pitch

Yaw

Roll

Jetliner Engines

As the fully laden jetliner accelerates down the runway, the engines deliver their maximum power. It is now that their reliability is all-important. Tucked into the seat in front of each passenger is a brochure which tells something of the story behind those engines.

The jetliner is powered by four Rolls Royce RB211's weighing four tonnes each and costing an incredible 1¼ million pounds each – together accounting for about one eighth of the total cost of the aircraft. On take-off the engines come under the greatest stress and deliver the equivalent power of 228 Ferrari Mondial 8 cars. At the cruising speed of 900 kph the power is cut back to one fifth, and on landing the engine thrust is reversed to assist braking. At every stage of flight an aircraft depends on the reliability and performance of its engines.

The cost of developing a new engine is enormous and it has to be tested rigorously before being allowed to go into service. So great was the cost of designing and testing the RB211, that in 1971 the British Government had to rescue Rolls Royce financially. This explains why, outside the USSR, there are only three major manufacturers of engines for large widebodied jetliners – Pratt and Whitney, General Electric and Rolls Royce. The rivalry between all three is very great, and with fuel costs rising, the efficiency of the engine is becoming increasingly important. For airlines fuel is now the single largest operating cost and in many cases, jetliners like the 747 and TriStar are offered to airlines with a choice of engines to suit their particular needs.

This engine is a Rolls Royce RB211, shown with its casings open for inspection during routine pre-flight checks. It is one of the makes of very high power turbofan engines used by modern jetliners. Although very complicated, it is designed in seven units to simplify and reduce the cost of maintenance.

The engine shown here is a turbofan. The air sucked in by the giant fan at the front (1) ▷ is expelled in two ways. Some air – about one seventh – is compressed in stages (2).

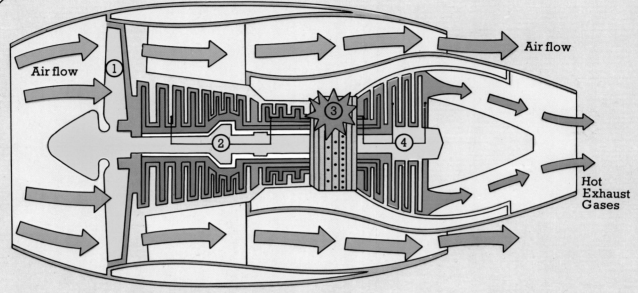

Air flow

Air flow

Hot Exhaust Gases

It is mixed with vaporized kerosene and ignited (3). Some exhaust gases provide a part of the forward thrust but most of the energy is used to power the turbines (4) ▷ which turn the compressors and the huge fan blades at the front. The remaining six-sevenths of the air is swallowed by the fan, increases in pressure and ▷ 'by-passes' the jet engine or 'core' completely. This provides the major thrust of the engine. The turbofan is more fuel-efficient and quieter than the turbojet.

The classic Boeing 707 was the first jetliner to use four podded jets leaving a 'clean' and efficient wing. This engine layout is used today by the 747. The Ilyushin IL-62 and the VC10 have two on each side of the rear fuselage.

Boeing 707-320C

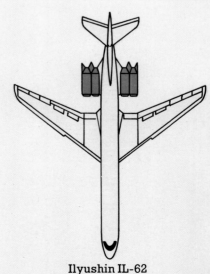

Ilyushin IL-62

14

Thrust reversers (1) give greatly increased braking power on landing. The exhaust gases are diverted by spoilers which deflect the gases forwards (2). The fan air which normally by-passes the engine core is reversed and expelled forwards.

Engine maintenance and the installation of new engines are made considerably easier by the location of the whole engine assembly as one unit or pod (3). This is suspended from a pylon (4) below and forward of the wing.

Fire detection and extinguishing is a vital safety factor in aircraft. Once a fire has been detected by heat sensors inside the engine, the fuel is cut off and the engine is stopped. Special chemicals are then sprayed into the engine.

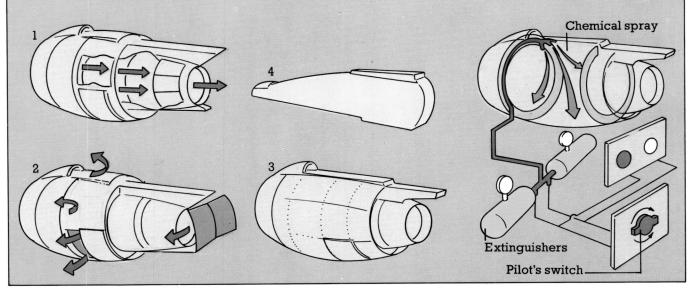

Chemical spray

Extinguishers

Pilot's switch

The Boeing 727, Trident, DC9 and BAC111 all have engines at the rear while the DC10, TriStar, TU154 all feature two jets under the wing and one at the rear. The new advanced technology wing of the A300 enables sufficient lift and power to be obtained from two large turbofans under the wing – and both the new Boeing 757 and 767 will follow this pattern.

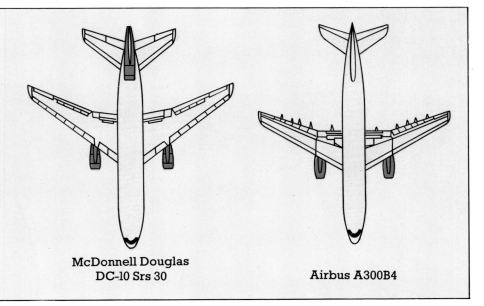

McDonnell Douglas
DC-10 Srs 30

Airbus A300B4

The Passenger Cabin

The jetliner has reached its cruising altitude of 10,000 metres and cruising speed of 900 km per hour. The passengers are now free to unfasten their safety belts and move around.

The passenger cabin layout consists of three sections. The 747 is unique in having two decks; on the upper deck, behind the flight crew there is the first class section. On the lower deck the business class section – for passengers who pay the full fare – is at the front; while behind is the much larger economy section for passengers who have special cheap rate tickets.

The stewards and stewardesses – 14 in all – are now busy around the galleys. Drinks, followed by dinner, the film and finally breakfast in the morning is the order of service. Individual headphones are distributed, and these, when plugged in to the arm of the seat – which also contains the reading light, fresh air control and call button – give a variety of inflight musical programmes.

Dinner is served on specially prepared trays, perhaps prawn cocktail, followed by a choice of roast chicken or braised steak with chocolate mousse to finish. The chicken and beef has been heated in the special microwave ovens in the galleys and it is hard to believe that a hot, three-course meal can be served while the jetliner is flying at this altitude and speed.

Dinner over, the cabin lights are dimmed, the blinds by the windows are drawn, the screens unfold and the film begins. Now, for the first time the cabin crew take it in turns to have a rest while the passengers snooze, or watch the film.

This is part of the economy class seating in a Boeing 747, with passengers seated ten abreast. The two aisles allow easy passenger movement and permit the cabin crew to move drink and food trolleys about. The overhead lockers are for hand luggage and the enclosed section at the rear of the picture, is one of several located in the aircraft which contain either galleys or toilets.

The seats shown here are from the first-class cabin. Passengers spend most of the flight in their seats. So not only must the seating be comfortable for a long period of time – but it must be strong enough to withstand the stresses of take-off and landing. Each seat is built to recline and must include the folding table and individual controls. All materials for the seat covers are flame resistant.

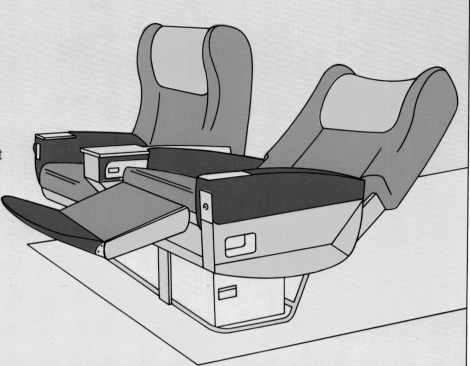

Galleys

Frozen precooked meals have overcome many of the difficulties of feeding passengers on long flights. When required they are heated in the ovens and loaded on to the trolleys before being served individually to passengers. Many aircraft such as the TriStar (shown here) store most of the food in an underfloor compartment which is connected by lift to the main cabin.

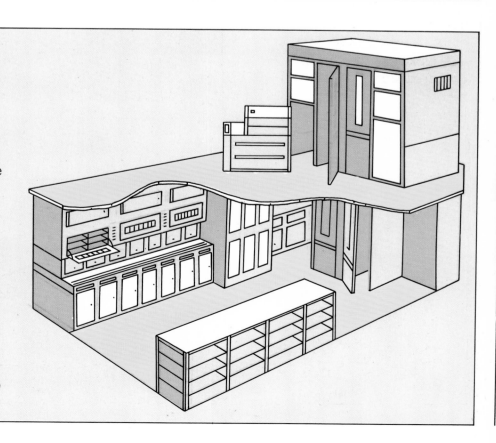

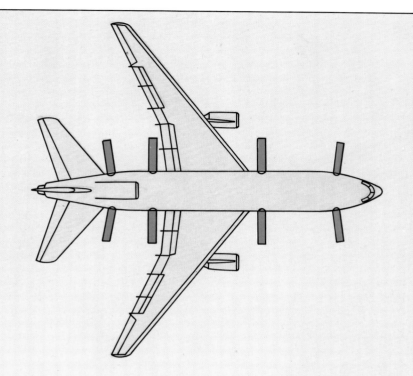

In the event of an accident passengers must get out of the aircraft as quickly as possible. Doors are provided right along both sides of the fuselage (in the TriStar shown there are four on each side). In each door is an inflatable chute down which the passengers slide to the ground, at the rate of one every 1½ seconds.

Stowed close to each seat is an inflatable lifejacket, for use in the event of an emergency ditching at sea. The jacket has a bottle of compressed gas to inflate it rapidly, and an automatically activated light. It is designed so that the wearer will float in the upright position.

Built into the airliner's escape chute, or stowed near the emergency exits, are a sufficient number of liferafts for all on board the aircraft. Produced in varying sizes for different aircraft, these liferafts are self-inflating. They are supplied with standard items such as lifejackets, food, drinking water, medical gear, paddles, lifelines, sea anchor and a radio transmitter.

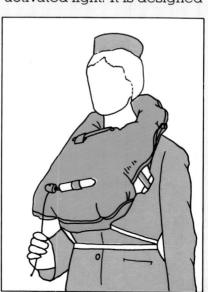

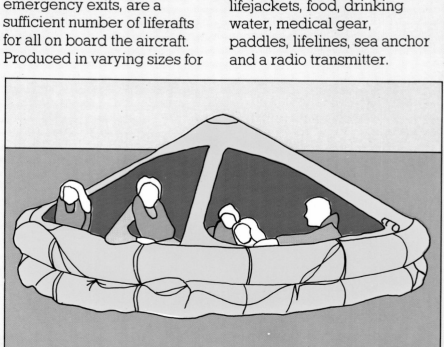

Jetliner Construction

In many respects a jetliner is like a flying hotel. On a long transatlantic flight the 370 passengers expect to be carried in comfort; they have to be entertained, fed and generally looked after. On shorter flights and with smaller aircraft, the same facilities have to be offered but over a much shorter period of time.

Unlike a hotel however, a jetliner travels at speed and at very high altitudes. The construction of the aircraft is immensely complex, and has to be strong enough to withstand the stresses of air turbulence, take-off and landing. Temperatures may vary from 40°C on the ground to −52°C in the air and special aluminium copper alloys have been designed to withstand such temperature changes and yet be light and strong.

Passengers and crew are housed in the tubelike fuselage. At the cruising altitude of 10,000 metres, the air contains so little oxygen that it becomes very difficult to breathe. The fuselage is then specially pressurized to give a normal air pressure inside even though outside the pressure may be much less. The wings are built to support the whole weight of the aircraft whilst in flight; they provide the mounting points for the engines and have the fuel tanks built into them. At the rear, the tail unit stabilizes the aircraft in pitch and yaw. Under the floor of the main deck is the freight and baggage hold, a number of the aircraft control systems, and space for the aircraft's landing gear.

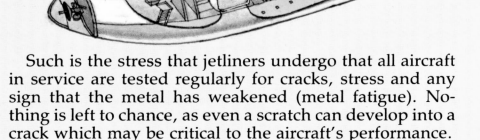

Such is the stress that jetliners undergo that all aircraft in service are tested regularly for cracks, stress and any sign that the metal has weakened (metal fatigue). Nothing is left to chance, as even a scratch can develop into a crack which may be critical to the aircraft's performance.

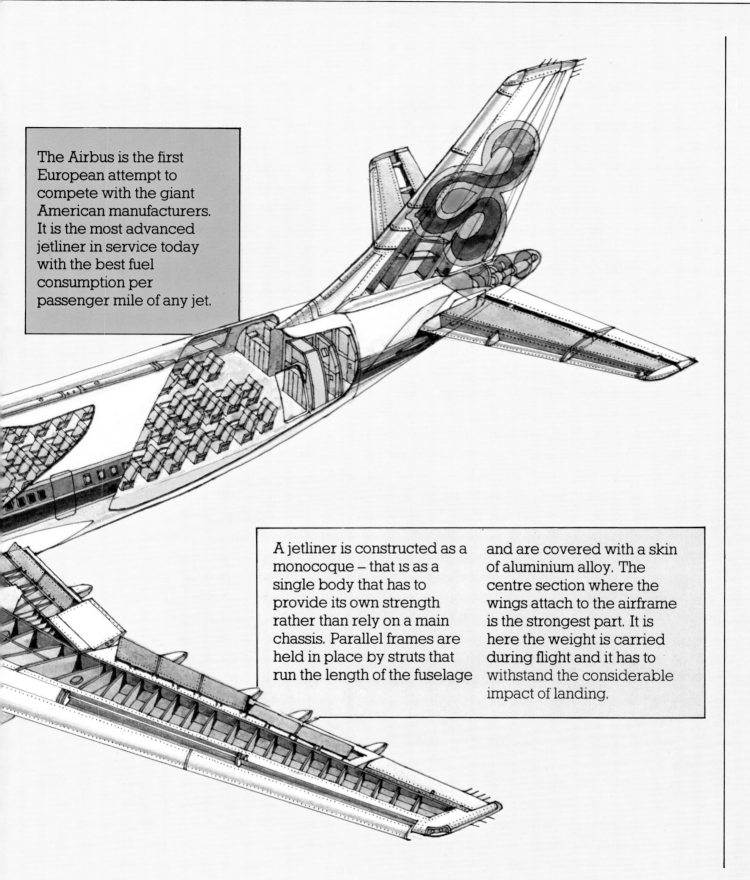

The Airbus is the first European attempt to compete with the giant American manufacturers. It is the most advanced jetliner in service today with the best fuel consumption per passenger mile of any jet.

A jetliner is constructed as a monocoque – that is as a single body that has to provide its own strength rather than rely on a main chassis. Parallel frames are held in place by struts that run the length of the fuselage and are covered with a skin of aluminium alloy. The centre section where the wings attach to the airframe is the strongest part. It is here the weight is carried during flight and it has to withstand the considerable impact of landing.

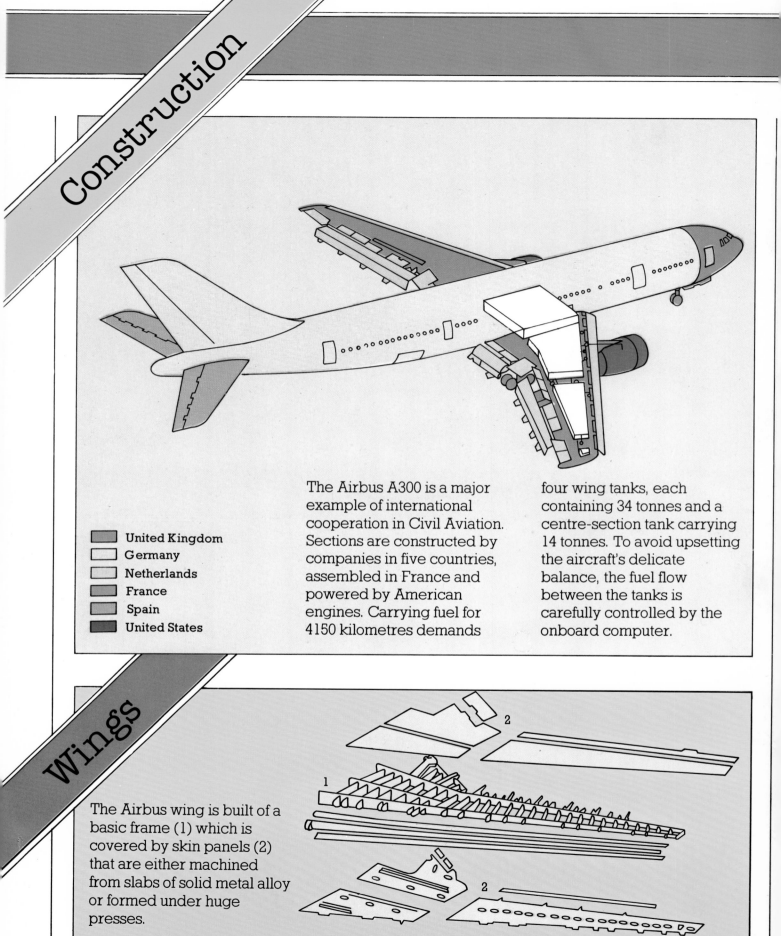

United Kingdom
Germany
Netherlands
France
Spain
United States

The Airbus A300 is a major example of international cooperation in Civil Aviation. Sections are constructed by companies in five countries, assembled in France and powered by American engines. Carrying fuel for 4150 kilometres demands four wing tanks, each containing 34 tonnes and a centre-section tank carrying 14 tonnes. To avoid upsetting the aircraft's delicate balance, the fuel flow between the tanks is carefully controlled by the onboard computer.

Wings

The Airbus wing is built of a basic frame (1) which is covered by skin panels (2) that are either machined from slabs of solid metal alloy or formed under huge presses.

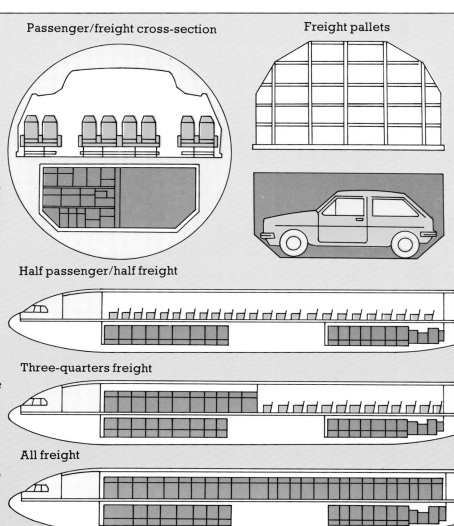

Passenger/freight cross-section

Freight pallets

Half passenger/half freight

Three-quarters freight

All freight

All jetliners today are built to take both freight and passengers. Some versions of modern jetliners, for example the 747C, are designed to carry freight in place of some, or even all, of the passengers. The seats can be stripped from the cabin to make more freight space and they are equipped with an extra large cargo loading door either in the nose section which swings up or in the fuselage itself. Freight can be carried in containers or made up into packages on standard pallets. Special loads can also be fitted in.

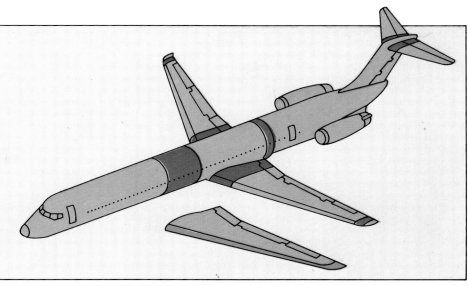

The DC9 Super 80 jetliner is 'stretched' to increase passenger capacity. Additional sections are built into the fuselage and wings and more powerful engines are fitted.

Flightdeck

Perched high in the nose in a special compartment is the flightdeck – the nerve centre of the aircraft. The first pilot (captain) and second pilot sit in the two forward seats. They share the basic flying and navigating functions and the controls for each are identical. The third crew member, facing to the right, has the primary responsibility of looking after the engines. There is also room for two observers when crew efficiency is being checked.

The huge array of instruments tell the crew about every aspect of the aircraft's altitude and performance, and deal with all aspects of the engine and fuel situation as well as a host of internal and external factors. There are also many computerized electronic systems for communications, navigation, flight and voice recording, radar and automatic flight control. All of these are duplicated or even triplicated for safety.

The autopilot is used for much of the flight although at least one pilot is always monitoring the systems and ready to take over normal control at any time. By feeding into a computer all the relevant flight details, the autopilot is able to make directional changes on its own. More importantly, fully automatic landings can be made at certain airports when visibility is reduced to a minimum due to fog or bad weather.

The TriStar flightdeck: 1 Overhead switch panel; 2 Flight instruments panel; 3 Control column; 4 Rudder and brake pedals; 5 Throttles; 6 Central console for weather radar controls, radio equipment and autopilot; 7 Flight Engineer's panel containing fuel-usage instruments and engine monitoring systems.

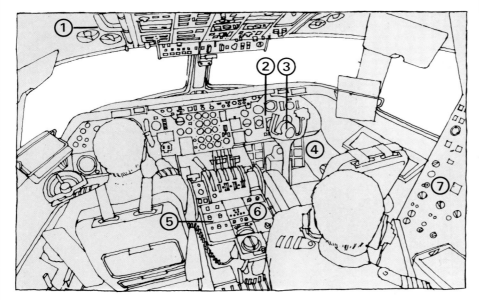

A feature of the new Boeing 767 is its revolutionary flight-deck. The performance of the aircraft will be monitored by as few as nine TV screens rather than the mass of dials used today. The number of flight crew required to fly the aircraft may be reduced from three to two and the aircraft's attitude, course, flight performance, fuel, engines and systems will be displayed in a number of coded colours.

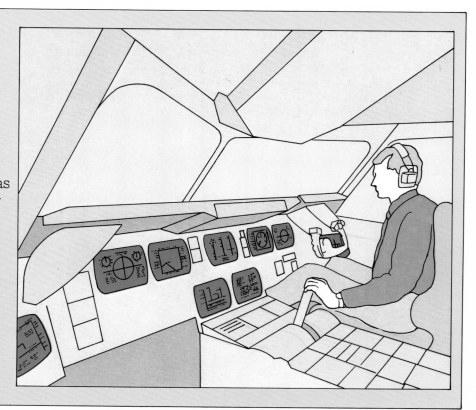

The Dials

Apart from the altimeter, a simple indicator showing the aircraft's height above sea level, the pilot has three important flight instruments. The air speed indicator (1), showing the aircraft's speed in knots, the horizontal situation indicator (2), giving the aircraft's position in relation to various navigation beams, and the attitude director (3) which confirms the aircraft is flying straight and level.

1
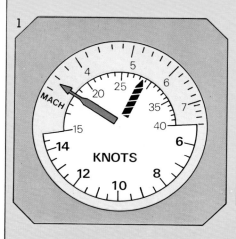

2
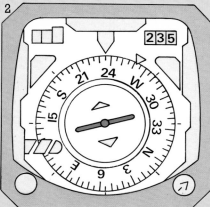

3
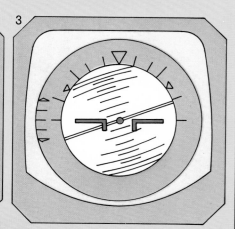

One hour before the flight the crew meet to finalize the flight plan. With the aid of computers they are able to obtain a printout (1) of all the relevant information – the number of passengers, the freight, baggage, fuel and above all the forecast weather conditions. The flight path chosen will be the best available – shortest, quickest and most economical. Once agreed, the captain signs his acceptance of the plan which is then forwarded by teleprinter to the traffic control centres along the route.

On most short and medium flights, aircraft fly along airways which are controlled by radio beacons, each of which has its own radio code and frequency. By picking up these signals the crew can pinpoint their position by comparing it with the extensive maps (2) they have been given at the flight briefing.

Today, advanced navigation systems do not rely on beacons or airways. The Boeing 767 for example, will fly *above* busy airways and avoid traffic bottlenecks.

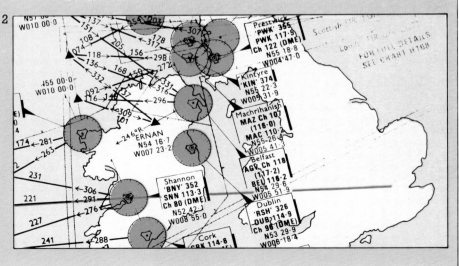

Air Traffic Control

Like all modern airliners, the 747 can be navigated with pinpoint accuracy by its inbuilt systems, but its safety in the air, especially with regard to the movements of other aircraft, remains the responsibility of worldwide Air Traffic Control (ATC) systems.

Every airliner is fitted with a transponder – a radio transmitter that gives out a four figure number – to identify it on ATC's radar screens. In large windowless rooms (below) the controllers watch the movement of aircraft along the prescribed airways 16 km wide and stretching up to 23,000 metres. Each controller tries to ensure that within his sector no aircraft passes within 5½ km of another, or that when this is impossible the two aircraft are separated vertically by at least 300 metres. As the airliner moves from sector to sector the pilot is kept informed of relevant weather and other conditions.

Nearing the airport, the flightcrew report in to the approach controller in the control tower (right). If possible, this controller directs the aircraft straight on to its landing course, if this is impossible he orders the aircraft into a 'stack' or holding pattern.

The approach controller moves the aircraft out of the stack and hands over to the controller in the Aircraft Control Tower who guides the aircraft towards the runway, making sure that there is an interval of at least three minutes between the aircraft in front. The aircraft is watched closely from the control tower until it has landed and turned off the runway.

Civil airspace divisions:
1 Above 15,000m, controlled airspace monitoring all traffic;
2 above 8000m, monitoring traffic approaching airport;
3 below 8000m, monitoring traffic landing and taking off.

Finding the direction is not as difficult as fixing one's exact position in the air. Although compasses and gyroscopes are still carried they have been superseded by a number of systems. VOR – very high frequency omnidirectional range is the most used radio system. By transmitting a signal to a VOR beacon and measuring the time of the reply – exact distances can be gauged. INS – Inertial Navigation System – represents a huge advance in navigation. The system measures every slightest movement of the aircraft and shows the exact position throughout the flight.

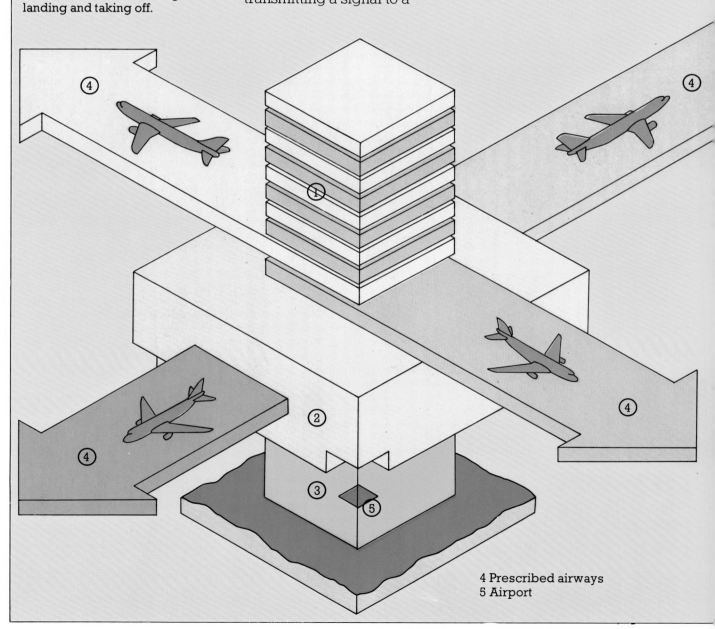

4 Prescribed airways
5 Airport

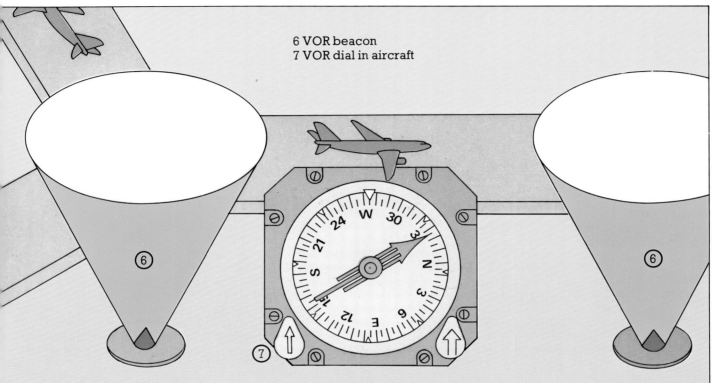

6 VOR beacon
7 VOR dial in aircraft

Before and after take-off each aircraft is under the direct guidance of the Airport Traffic Control. When clear of the airport the captain is directed on to his flight plan and airway. These aerial motorways defined by the beacons at regular points are controlled in large regional centres with the aid of giant radar scanners. Civil airspace is divided into three main blocks – above 15,000 metres for supersonic and business jets – between 15,000 and 8,000 metres for ordinary civil jetliners and below 8,000 metres for propeller driven aircraft

All aircraft travel at the same speed in each block and are kept well apart.

The most advanced navigation system in the world is Omega. This system is based on a worldwide network of very low frequency (VLF) radio transmissions from only eight specially located stations. All the transmissions are very carefully synchronized, and comparison of each signal received, made possible only by an airliner's onboard computer, gives the aircraft's exact position.

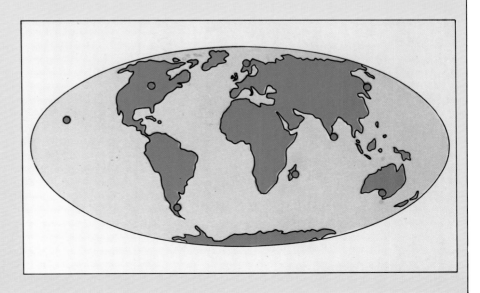

Landing

The autopilot picks up the two sets of beams from the Instrument Landing System (ILS) as the jetliner approaches the specific runway along the glidepath. The captain has chosen to make an automatic landing even though the visibility is good, because it is more consistent and therefore safer than a manual landing. Although the crew do not need to touch the controls until the aircraft is on the runway they watch very carefully the reading from the instruments and check the aircraft's descent against the Visual Approach Slope Indicators (VASI) on each side of the runway.

Touchdown at Frankfurt as dawn breaks over the airport complex. This flight is one of 900 in and out of Frankfurt every day.

In the passenger cabin, the travellers and cabin staff are securely strapped in to their seats; all cigarettes are extinguished and the music system is playing. The descent is calm and controlled. The only change in attitude is about 20 metres from the ground when the pilot brings up the aircraft's nose to slow its approach speed. The main wheels gently thump down, followed quickly by the nosewheel. The brakes are applied and the aircraft turns off the runway and rolls to a halt. A perfect three-point landing.

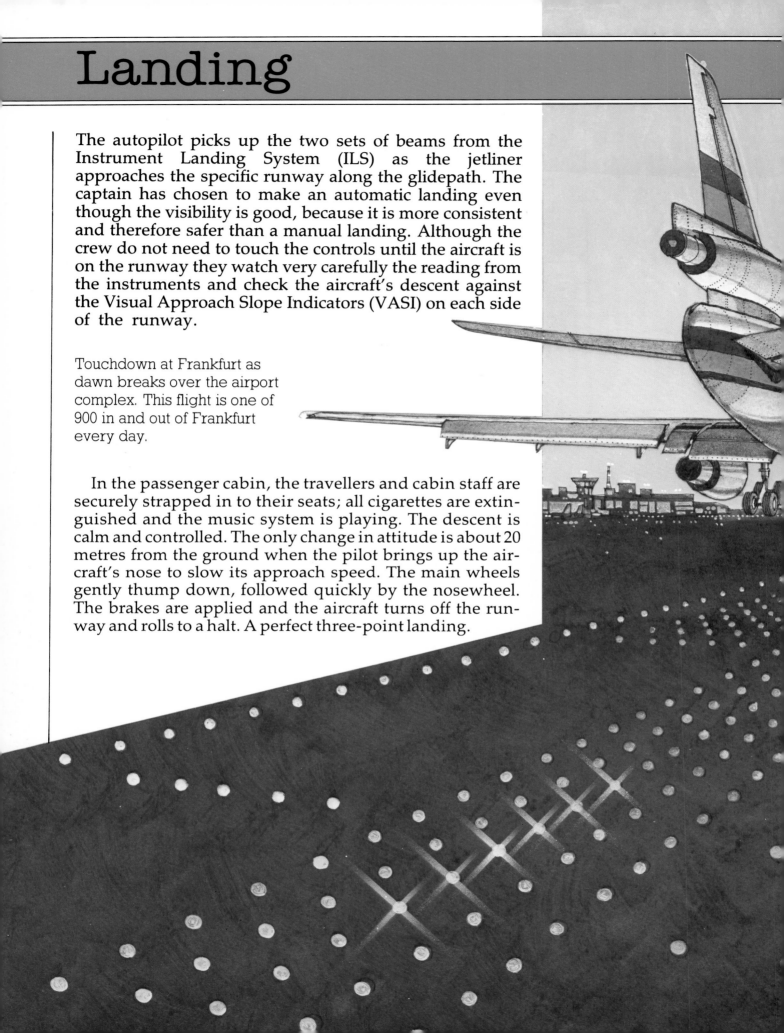

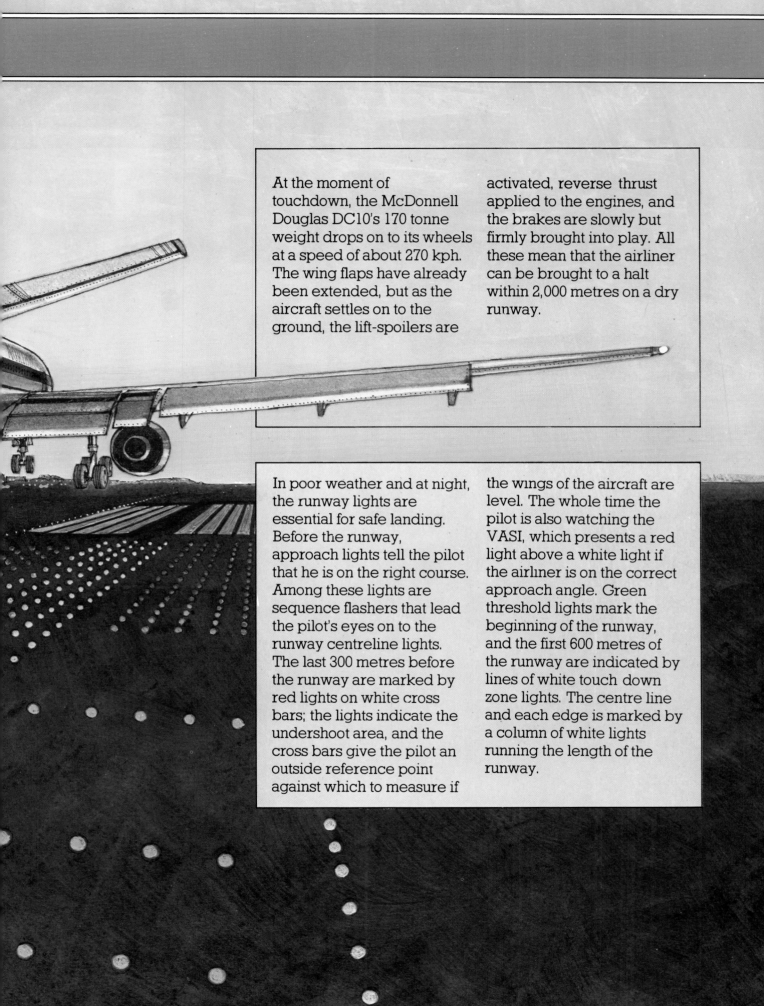

At the moment of touchdown, the McDonnell Douglas DC10's 170 tonne weight drops on to its wheels at a speed of about 270 kph. The wing flaps have already been extended, but as the aircraft settles on to the ground, the lift-spoilers are activated, reverse thrust applied to the engines, and the brakes are slowly but firmly brought into play. All these mean that the airliner can be brought to a halt within 2,000 metres on a dry runway.

In poor weather and at night, the runway lights are essential for safe landing. Before the runway, approach lights tell the pilot that he is on the right course. Among these lights are sequence flashers that lead the pilot's eyes on to the runway centreline lights. The last 300 metres before the runway are marked by red lights on white cross bars; the lights indicate the undershoot area, and the cross bars give the pilot an outside reference point against which to measure if the wings of the aircraft are level. The whole time the pilot is also watching the VASI, which presents a red light above a white light if the airliner is on the correct approach angle. Green threshold lights mark the beginning of the runway, and the first 600 metres of the runway are indicated by lines of white touch down zone lights. The centre line and each edge is marked by a column of white lights running the length of the runway.

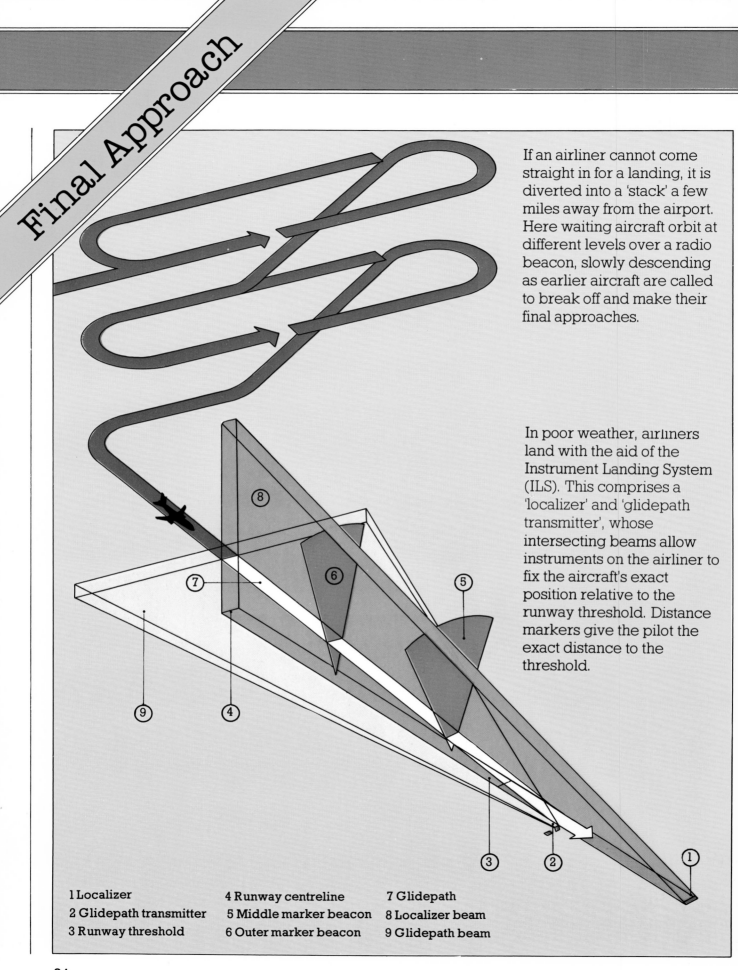

If an airliner cannot come straight in for a landing, it is diverted into a 'stack' a few miles away from the airport. Here waiting aircraft orbit at different levels over a radio beacon, slowly descending as earlier aircraft are called to break off and make their final approaches.

In poor weather, airliners land with the aid of the Instrument Landing System (ILS). This comprises a 'localizer' and 'glidepath transmitter', whose intersecting beams allow instruments on the airliner to fix the aircraft's exact position relative to the runway threshold. Distance markers give the pilot the exact distance to the threshold.

1 Localizer
2 Glidepath transmitter
3 Runway threshold
4 Runway centreline
5 Middle marker beacon
6 Outer marker beacon
7 Glidepath
8 Localizer beam
9 Glidepath beam

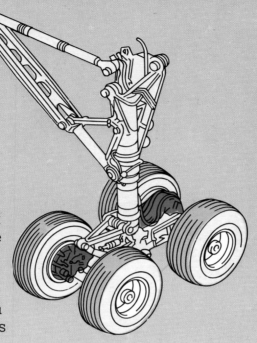

Each leg of the undercarriage is attached at its upper end to the airframe and carries at its lower end one or more wheels (and associated brake systems) that connect the aircraft with the ground. The legs, wheels and specially designed tyres take enormous loads at take-off and landing. Mainwheel legs of large jetliners now usually have a four-wheel combination or bogie, hinged so that the two rear wheels touch down before the two front wheels. The system for retraction (usually sideways into the under surface of the wing or the lower fuselage) uses a highpower hydraulic jack. Shock absorbers use a mixture of oil and air to cushion the landing.

Just after touchdown, the pilot's main job is to hold the airliner on the runway centreline. The engines are in reverse thrust, the brakes are on, and the flaps and spoilers are fully extended to produce as much drag as possible. The rudder is used to keep the aircraft in the centre until speed has dropped to the point where the pilot can steer with the nosewheel.

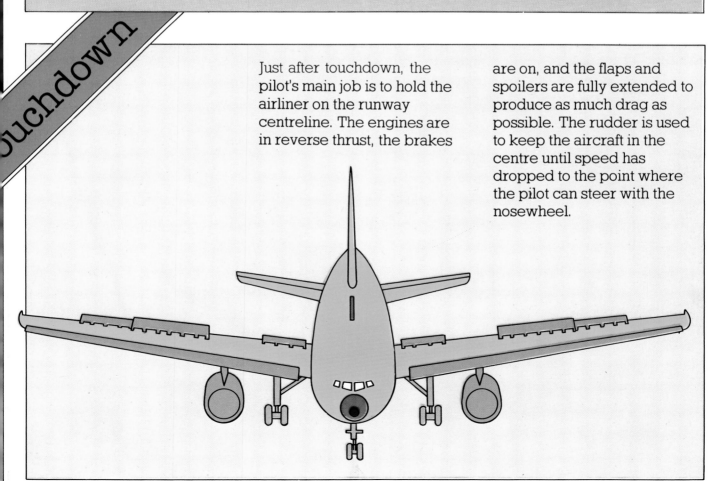

Glossary

Ailerons
Small flaps on the wings which can be extended on take-off to increase the size of the wings and thus give the aircraft maximum lift.

Airspeed Indicator
An instrument which measures the speed of the aircraft.

Altimeter
An instrument which tells the pilot how high the plane is above sea level.

Autopilot
Computerized electronic system which can fly the plane, adjust course and land without manual control by the pilot.

Drag
The air's resistance to moving objects.

Elevator
The horizontal control surface on the tailplane which controls climb or descent.

Engine Thrust
The forward propulsion given to an aircraft by its jet engines.

Flap
A movable part on the wing surface which, when extended on take-off or landing, increases lift or drag.

Fuselage
The body of the aircraft.

Glidepath
The sloping course along which an aircraft comes in to land.

Horizontal Situation Indicator
An instrument which gives the aircraft's position in relation to various navigational radio beams.

INS (Inertial Navigational System)
A system which measures the slightest movement of an aircraft in the air and shows its exact position throughout a flight.

Monocoque
A single body structure that has to provide its own strength rather than relying on a central chassis.

Omega
The most advanced navigational system in the world for aircraft. It is based on a worldwide network of low frequency radio transmitters.

Pitch
The up and down movement of an aircraft which can be controlled by elevators on the tailplane.

Roll
The tilting of an aircraft from side to side which can be controlled by means of the wing flaps.

Spoiler
The control surface on the aircraft's wings that destroys lift by disturbing air-flow over the wing. In use they increase drag to slow the aircraft.

Stack
The holding position given to an aircraft by Air Traffic Control while it is waiting to land at an airport.

Stall
Loss of lift due to an acute wing angle, often caused by insufficient speed.

Thrust reversers
Parts of an aircraft engine which cause the exhaust gases to be deflected forward to give greater braking power for landing.

Transponder
A radio transmitter, fitted to all aircraft, which gives out a four figure number identifying the plane to Air Traffic Control.

Turbofan
A jet engine in which most of the air drawn into the engine passes the core and is expelled as a cold air stream. This helps engine cooling and makes it quieter and increases fuel efficiency.

VASI (Visual Approach Slope Indicators)
Signal lights at the sides of the runway which tell an aircraft about to land if it is on the correct approach course.

VOR (Very High Frequency Omnidirectional Range)
A system by which radio beams are transmitted from an aircraft to a beacon on the ground in order to calculate the plane's exact position in the air.

Yaw
The swivelling movement of an aircraft to right or left which can be controlled by the rudder on the tailplane fin.

Index

Aladdin Books would like to thank the following for their valuable help in the production of this book:

Ted Duggan (Public Relations Manager, British Airways); Jenny Atkinson (British Airports Authority); Civil Aviation Authority (Library and Photographic staffs); Atlanta International Airport; British Aerospace; Boeing International Corporation; Chubb Fire Security Ltd; Eastern Airlines; *Flight* Magazine; General Electric; ICI Paints Division; Lockheed Manufacturing; Lufthansa; McDonnell Douglas Corporation; Pratt & Whitney Aircraft; RFD Inflatables Ltd; Rolls Royce Ltd.